Table of Contents

About the Writers

Julia Olson got her start teaching piano in Utah, where she also taught preschool at a private school that emphasized learning through music. Since then, she has taught private piano lessons as well as early childhood music and group piano classes in California and Illinois. She is a member of the National Music Teachers Association and the Early Childhood Music and Movement Association. In addition to maintaining a piano studio with children of all ages, Julia directs children's choirs in her community.

Kevin Olson is an active pianist, composer, and member of the piano faculty at Utah State University, where he teaches piano literature, pedagogy, and accompanying courses. In addition to his collegiate teaching responsibilities, Kevin directs the Utah State Youth Conservatory, which provides weekly group and private piano instruction to more than 200 pre-college, community students. Before teaching at Utah State, he was on the faculty at Elmhurst College near Chicago and Humboldt State University in northern California.

He also writes and edits music for The FJH Music Company, which he joined as a writer in 1994. Many of the needs of his own piano students have inspired a diverse collection of books and solos he has published of original music and instructional material. Kevin received his bachelor's and master's degrees in music composition and theory from Brigham Young University, and holds a Doctorate of Education from National-Louis University.

Kevin and Julia live in Logan, Utah with their four children: Skyler, Casey, Aubery, and Wesley.

Notes to the Teacher

The Perfect Start for Solo Playing is a collection of solo pieces that can be used in correlation with each unit of *The Perfect Start for Note Reading,* or as a separate early elementary level solo book.

The solo pieces in this book offer sequential reinforcement of the notes students are learning at this level, and introduce students to the concept of playing with expression and artistry. Students should be encouraged to "tell a story" through the music as they follow the many changes in dynamics, tempo, pedaling, articulation, and octave shifts. By following all musical markings on the pages, students will develop a sense of artistic style from their earliest years at the piano. All artistic markings in this book, such as 8va and pedal, are optional if teachers determine that they are too difficult for a student's level of performance.

It is our hope that students will enjoy learning and performing the pieces in this book, as they discover the joys of playing musically at the piano.

Kevin and Julia Olson

Blowing Bubbles

After you are comfortable with this piece, try playing with **R.H.** finger **2** on **C.**

Goblin Games

Allegro

Watch the gob - lins | play a game | on the moun - tain - side;

5 8va (one octave higher)

First they shout, and | then they sing, and | then they run and | hide.

9 *Play as written.* .... 8va (one octave higher)

One, two, three, be - | hind a tree. | Four, five, six, they | pick up sticks.

13 *Play as written.*

Then they call each | oth - er names | in their gob - lin | games.

After you are comfortable with this piece, try playing with **R.H.** finger **3** on **D.**

All Aboard!

After you are comfortable with this piece, try playing with **R.H.** finger **2** on **C.**

Ferris Wheel Ride

Andante

8va (one octave higher) — — — — — — — —

p

15ma (two octaves higher) — — — — — — — — — — — — — — — —   *Fine*

Play as written.

Rid - ing on a   Fer - ris wheel,   way up in the   air,

f

(no pedal)

D.C. al Fine

At the top, I'm   up so high, but   I'm not e - ven   scared.

D.C. al Fine means to return to the beginning and play until you see *Fine*. *Fine* means "end."

After you are comfortable with this piece, try playing with **R.H.** finger **2** on **C**.

FJH2

A Nose That Blows and Blows

After you are comfortable with this piece, try playing with **R.H.** fingers **2** and **4** on **C** and **E.**

Tiny Goldfish

Curved lines connecting different notes are called *slurs*. When you see a slur, connect the notes by playing smoothly *(legato)*.

After you are comfortable with this piece, try playing with **R.H.** finger **2** on **C.**

Shooting Star

After you are comfortable with this piece, try playing with **R.H.** finger **1** on **D.**

FJH21

Scary Dreams

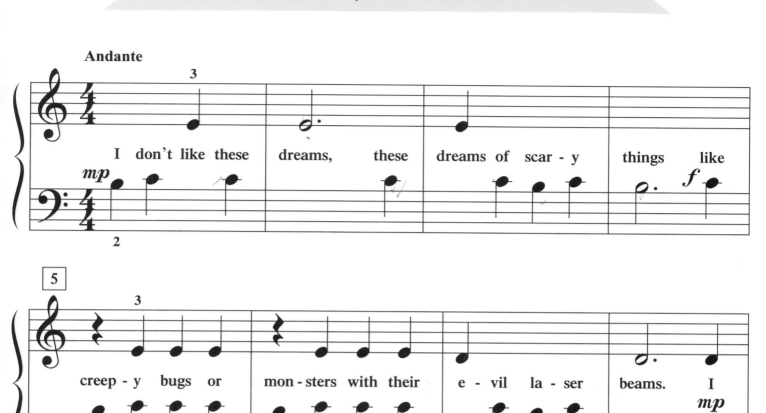

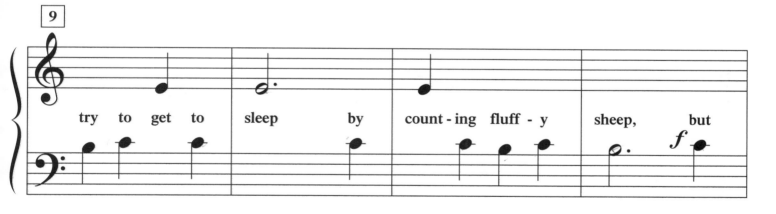

Play the lowest note on the piano. 8va⌐

After you are comfortable with this piece, try playing with **R.H.** finger **2** on **E.**

H2189

13

Grumpy Grampa

Play staccato notes short and detached.

With a bad attitude!

8va (L.H. one octave lower) – – – – – – –

Play L.H. as written.

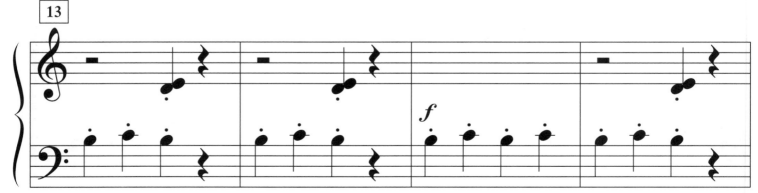

8va (L.H. one octave lower) – – – – – – –

FJH21

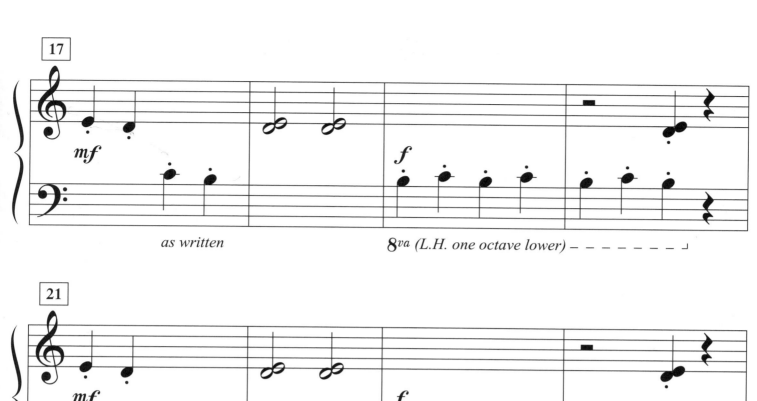

as written

8*va* (L.H. one octave lower) – – – – – – – –

as written

8*va* (L.H. one octave lower) – – – – – – – –

as written

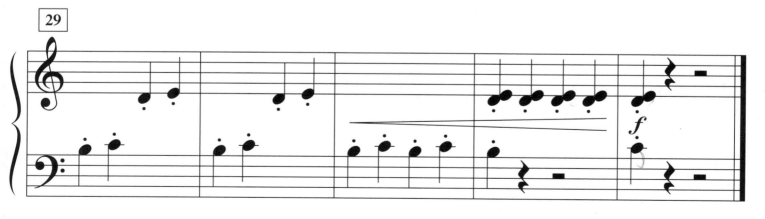

The crescendo mark means to gradually play louder.

After you are comfortable with this piece, try playing with **R.H.** finger **1** on **D.**

Unit 4

Peacock

⌢ The fermata mark means to hold the note longer than usual.

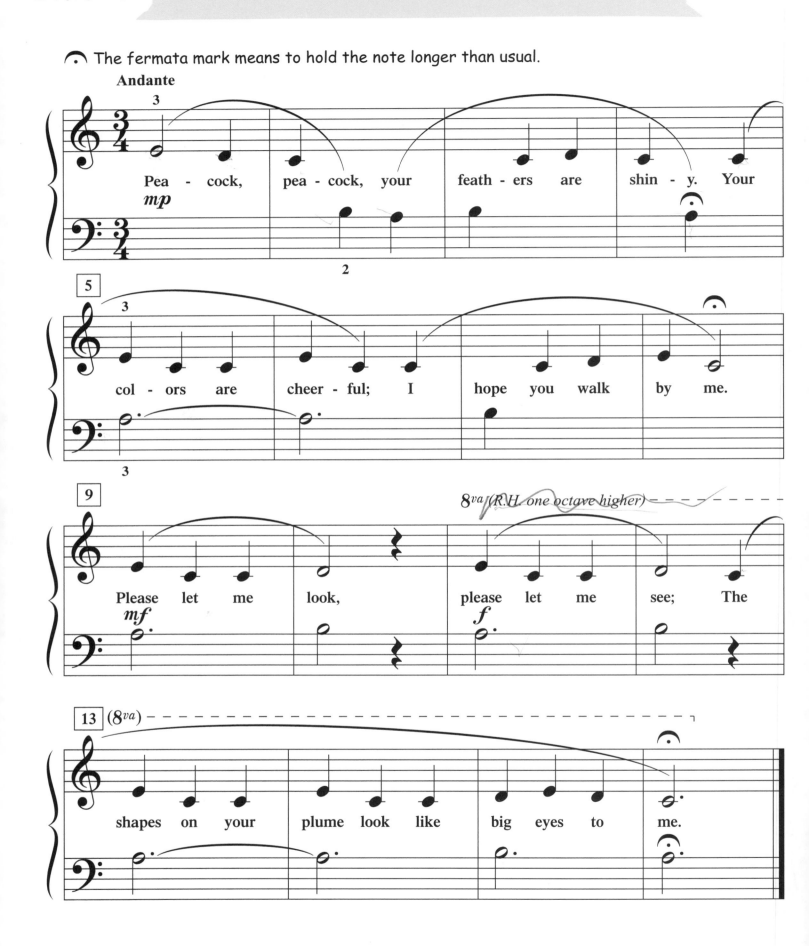

After you are comfortable with this piece, try playing with **L.H.** finger **1** on **B.**

I Have to Sneeze

After you are comfortable with this piece, try playing with **R.H.** fingers **1** and **2** on **D** and **E.**

Storm's Coming

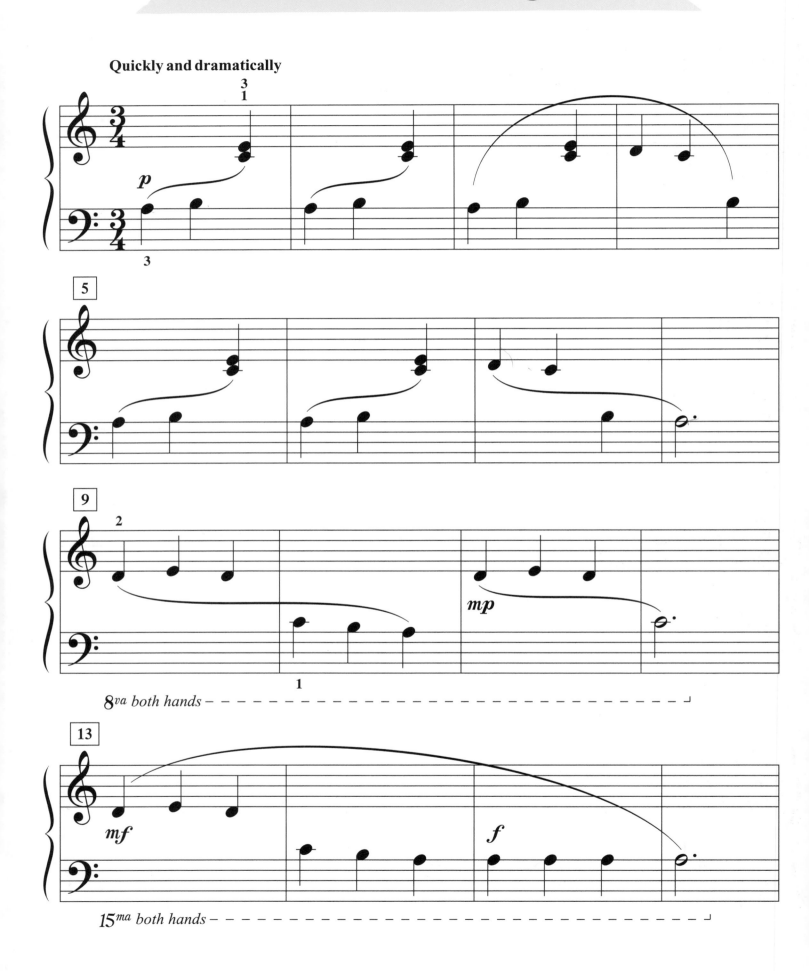

FJH218

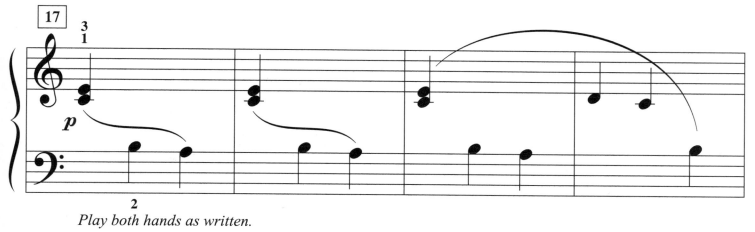

17

Play both hands as written.

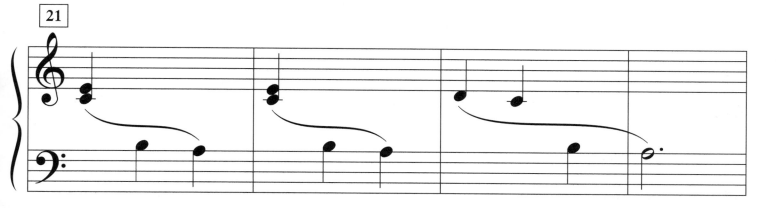

21

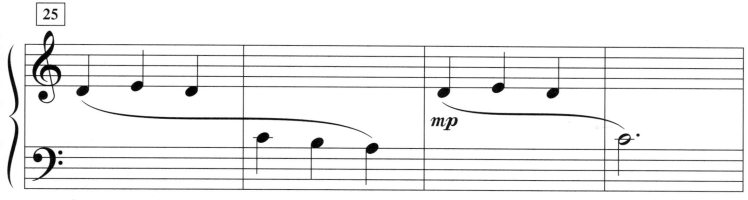

25

8ᵛᵃ both hands –

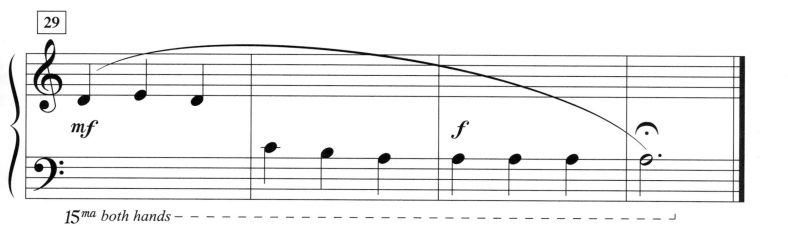

29

15ᵐᵃ both hands –

Be a Friend

After you are comfortable with this piece, try playing with **R.H.** finger **2** on **E.**

Big Old Hippo

Play slowly, in any low octave of the piano.

After you are comfortable with this piece, try playing with **R.H.** finger **2** on **E.**

Morning Mist

FJH21

After you are comfortable with this piece, try playing with **L.H.** finger **2** on **A.**

The End of a Rainbow

Tiptoes

After you are comfortable with this piece, try playing with **R.H.** finger **1** on **D.**

Traffic Sounds

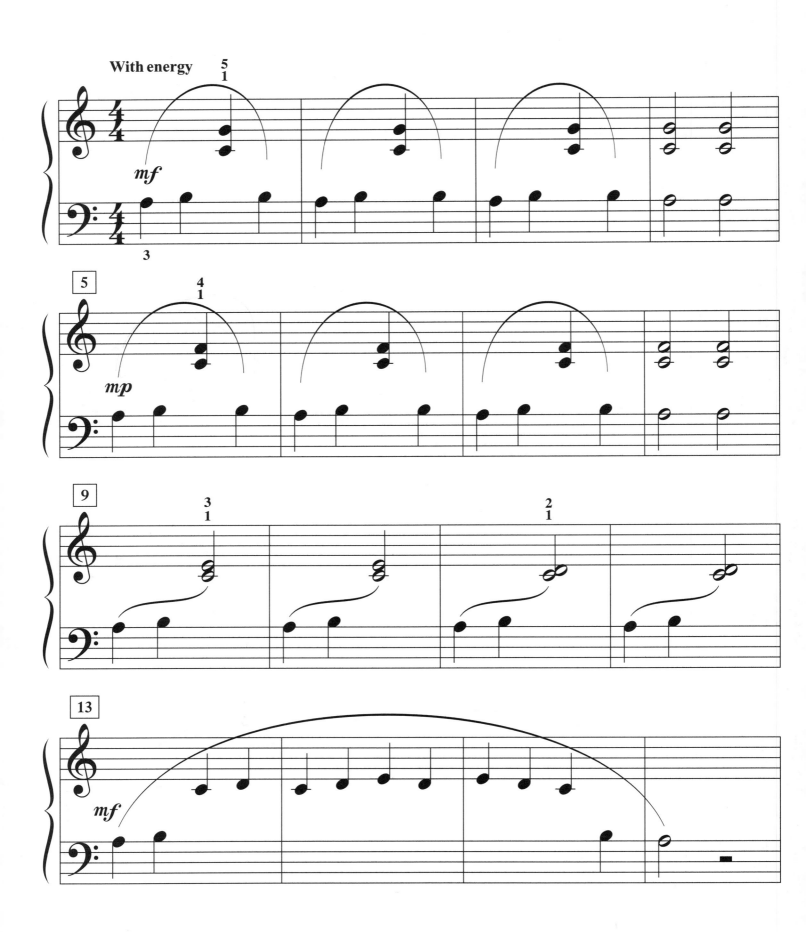

Out in the City

Allegro

Out in the cit - y, I see all the trains; I

see all the tax - is and hear all the planes. This

cit - y is cra - zy, but I think it's great, 'cause

it is the big - gest in all of the state!

Play the lowest C on the piano. 8va

After you are comfortable with this piece, try playing with **R.H.** finger **2** on **E.**

Snowflakes on My Tongue

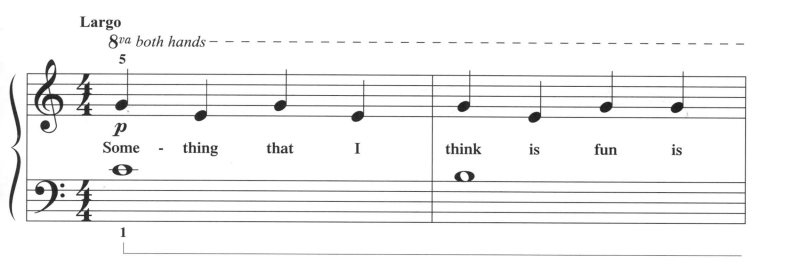

Little Drops of Rain on the Window Pane

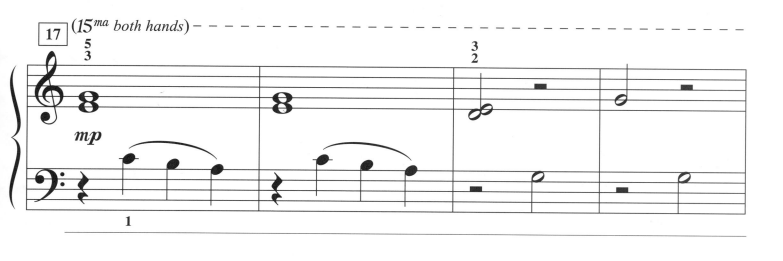

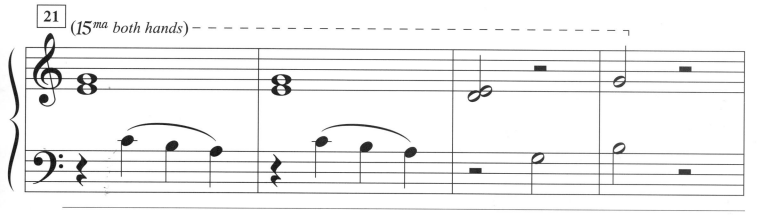

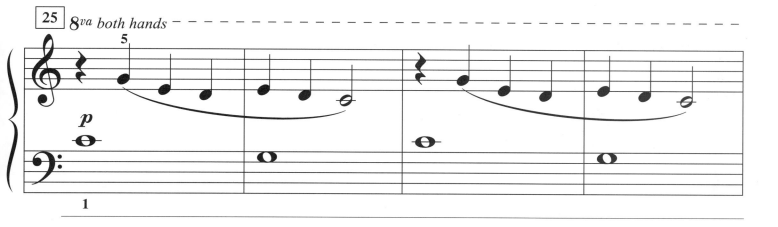

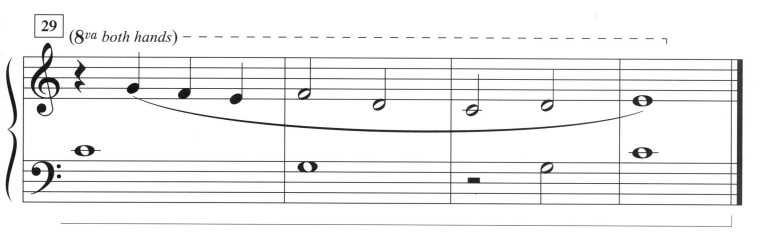

Barn Owl

Brand-New Socks

Fiddle Tune